Teacher's Handbook

SRA Reading Laboratory® 2c

Don H. Parker, Ph.D.

SRA/McGraw-Hill
Columbus, Ohio

The SQR study technique is an adaptation of "SQ3R Method" from EFFECTIVE STUDY,
4th Edition by Francis P. Robinson. Copyright © 1961, 1970 by Francis P. Robinson.
Copyright © 1941, 1946 by Harper & Row, Publishers, Inc. Reprinted by permission of
Harper & Row, Publishers, Inc.

Printed in the United States of America.

Send all inquiries to:
SRA/McGraw-Hill
250 Old Wilson Bridge Road
Suite 310
Worthington, OH 43085

0-02-687323-0

1 2 3 4 5 6 7 8 9 DBH 00 99 98 97 96

Contents

Many years ago, I discovered the importance of student self-determination as I worked with a seventh-grade class of thirty-five boys and girls averaging two years below grade level in reading. Within that group, standardized reading achievement test scores ranged from reading-grade levels three through ten. We set out to improve the situation, and from our experience we developed a "multi-level, self-operating" method of learning that would later become known as the SRA READING LABORATORY® program. The students controlled their own learning. My job was that of helper when needed—and it was a deeply satisfying one.

In the process, I learned more about myself. I discovered that I really *wanted* to help each one. I found myself willing to listen as never before. I really *cared* to give my energy in the different ways each one needed it. I also observed John and Maria and Tom and Ann and all the rest becoming more aware of their uniqueness, counting individual differences not as calamities, but as the very things that made each one *somebody*.

I learned something else. Each time a student confronts a learning exercise, he or she approaches it from one of dozens of possible ways—ways possible only to him or her because of the life experiences that each one has had up to that moment. When you recognize this, you honor a student's creativity and foster his or her growth.

We also found that because our systematic approach produced greater skill learning in less time than ordinary methods, there was time left over for free reading that each student could choose. And even more exciting, boys and girls—sparked by their reading—found creative ways of sharing individual life experiences. In this I only needed to be a catalyst, and they took off!

The SRA READING LABORATORY program still produces measurable results in terms of standardized reading test scores in classrooms throughout the world. (My seventh-graders gained a year and a half in reading comprehension in three months.) I invite you now to discover what can happen when you and your students experience multilevel learning.

DON H. PARKER, Ph.D.

A WEALTH OF GOOD READING

◆ For close to forty years, teachers have been aware of the strengths of the various SRA READING LABORATORY kits—how they provide individualized skills instruction, permit independent work, promote students' sense of responsibility, and let each student move at his or her own rate, according to individual ability. But there is another aspect of the Laboratory kits that deserves to be stressed: the great quantity of *good reading* to be found in these kits.

The practice selections in an SRA READING LABORATORY kit are by no means just sterile skills exercises. They are short stories and articles that children actually *enjoy* reading. And they are sources of a great deal of incidental learning as well—about plants, animals, history, science, technology, discovery, fine arts, social institutions, sports, and our cultural heritage. Importantly, they range over past, present, and future perspectives.

Children don't just learn to "read better" by using the SRA READING LABORATORY program; they discover what it means to become readers. They gain pleasure, information, and—if the ultimate goal succeeds—a lifelong love of reading in all kinds of subject areas. They learn to read for a variety of purposes, and they discover what it is to read in a wide range of content areas. Appendix D at the back of this Handbook contains a complete listing and description of the many topics and interest areas, factual and fictional, that are covered in a typical SRA READING LABORATORY kit. We think you'll agree that good reading is not just an incidental aspect of the SRA READING LABORATORY system, but one of its principal attractions and strengths.

Every new edition of an SRA READING LABORATORY kit is updated and improved over previous editions. In this 1996 edition, the improvements include replacement of all selections deemed out-of-date. Many of the Power Builder stories have been replaced with brand-new selections accompanied by brand-new exercise material as well as more contemporary artwork, while other selections have been edited to bring them up-to-date.

CULTURAL LITERACY

◆ Although some selections in the 2a, 2b, and 2c kits have been replaced with more current material, the cultural literacy emphasis of the SRA READING LABORATORY program has been retained. Researchers are aware that *specific information* is as much a part of the literate reader's necessary equipment as are the skills of decoding, vocabulary, and structural analysis.

Virtually *any* interesting reading materials can be used to build skills, but materials relating to civilization's cultural heritage can provide the common storehouse of knowledge that can equip a student to read other materials aimed at the general reader with the fullest understanding and appreciation.*

In reading the Power Builder stories in the Laboratory kits, students will not only find plentiful entertainment, but they will also learn the origins and meanings of phrases such as "tilting at windmills." They will learn about the foolishness of holding grudges and the value of simplicity, determination, and helping others. They will read an eyewitness account of the Great Fire of London of 1666. They will also become familiar with the names of William Shakespeare, Edgar Allan Poe, Louisa May Alcott, Miguel de Cervantes, and Charlotte and Emily Brontë.

Of course, classic legend and literature are not the only sources that contribute to cultural literacy: science, technology, history, and even sports contribute to our common vocabulary of widely shared references. (And these subjects, too, are generously represented in the Laboratory kits.)

CULTURAL DIVERSITY

◆ In choosing and editing the new selections, SRA has not confined itself to an exclusively Western view of culture. SRA has ranged more widely over non-Western sources, drawing on the traditional tales of Asia, Africa, South America, and the Middle East. Students will learn how a tortoise in India discovered that sometimes it's wiser to keep silent. Students will also learn what happened when a husband and wife in China tried to double their fortunes, and how the parents of a beautiful daughter found that good fortune can be as close as your own backyard. SRA has also chosen stories and biographies of women and minorities, such as Judith Jamison, Maya Angelou, Bette Bao Lord, and Ida Guillory.

*In the United States, this idea was brought to the attention of the general public through Professor E. D. Hirsch, Jr.'s 1987 book, *Cultural Literacy: What Every American Needs to Know* (Houghton Mifflin).

OVERVIEW:
Getting to Know the Program

METHODS AND GOALS

◆ As a teacher, you know that students differ in *how fast* they learn as well as in *how much* they learn. In a typical classroom, there are many levels of learning. Hence the need exists for a schooling situation that can accommodate all those levels at the same time. The SRA READING LABORATORY program does precisely that.

The program meets the needs of slow, average, and superior learners by providing multilevel learning materials in one classroom package. It is a *complete* system offering individualized reading instruction to all your students. You need no additional materials or teaching assistance to operate it. In fact, it almost operates itself. After some initial training, students manage their own learning. They work independently, score their own work, and keep accurate accounts of their own progress.

The reading materials and associated skills exercises in any one Laboratory kit are organized into a series of color-designated difficulty levels that range both above and below the average for that grade or age group.

For example, the *Reading Laboratory 2c* kit (generally used with sixth-graders or eleven-year-olds) contains ten levels of high-interest materials, of which the simplest has a reading age of approximately nine. The most complex level has a reading age of approximately fourteen. The student who reads "below grade level" finds material that he or she can read right away. This removes the frustration of trying to read and understand material that is too difficult. At the same time, the more advanced child finds materials suited to his or her abilities. This removes the boredom that comes with reading materials that are too easy. Students progress according to their own abilities and at whatever pace is appropriate to each one.

You begin using the program in your classroom by giving a short six-minute test—the Starting Level Guide—to determine the color level in which each student should start. Even if your students have used the program before, it is still important to begin each school year with the Starting Level Guide and other introductory techniques in order to ensure the smooth working of the system.

Since students work individually and chart their own progress, you will have time to guide their work. You can give help when requested or when you think you should. Once a week, you'll want to have a brief individual

✔ *CHECKLIST*

GOALS OF THE READING LABORATORY PROGRAM:

❶ To develop comprehension, vocabulary, word analysis, and study skills

❷ To reinforce specific skills in which students may show a weakness

❸ To interest students in reading and to enlarge their specific knowledge, using a wide array of quality factual and fictional selections

❹ To develop the habit of independent work

❺ To develop the sense of personal responsibility as students take charge of their own learning program conference with each student. By studying the progress charts *with the student,* you can help the student evaluate his or her work. Then, you and the student can decide *together* if he or she is ready to move to the next color level.

Teachers are often surprised to see how much responsibility students can take for their own learning. The more you work with multilevel teaching and learning, the more you will see how many opportunities there are for building one-to-one relationships with your students. You will also see how students' self-esteem grows with learning.

The goals of the SRA READING LABORATORY program, then, go well beyond mere skills learning, although skills learning is certainly an important part of the whole. Five main goals are served by the various learning materials in the SRA READING LABORATORY kit and by the educational method and philosophy of the multilevel system.

If you would like to review in detail the reading skills on which the program is focused, simply turn to the Comprehension and Word Study Skills Charts in Appendix F of this Handbook. There, you can see at a glance the specific skills presented in each reading level and in each separate Power Builder within each level.

GETTING THE MOST OUT OF THE PROGRAM

◆ A clear understanding of four important points will help ensure that you and your students derive maximum benefit from the SRA READING LABORATORY system's pedagogical design. The author and publisher wish to give special emphasis to these points at the outset so that they will not be overlooked.

FOUR POINTS TO REMEMBER

Your **SRA READING LABORATORY kit** is a carefully structured system for teaching and developing essential skills and beneficial attitudes in an orderly and purposeful program. When treated as a regularly scheduled part of the classroom routine, making full use of Student Record Books, the Laboratory offers you an organized, systematic program that can significantly improve reading skills, study habits, and feelings of personal responsibility.

The **SRA READING LABORATORY program** has proven most effective when used over a fairly concentrated period of time instead of being spread out across the entire school year. The recommended schedule on page 16 calls for ten sessions (30 to 45 minutes long) spaced close together during the training phase and an independent phase consisting of Power Builder sessions and a Final Analysis session. When practice periods are kept close together, there is carryover learning from one day to the next. When practice periods are too far apart, carryover is lessened and students tend to forget not only the information learned, but even the procedures to follow. This is why a program of closely spaced sessions over a fairly concentrated period yields the optimum results.

It is not intended that every student work his or her way through *all* the **POWER BUILDERS** in a level, nor that a student work the Power Builders in strict sequence. Instead, a student selects (or is given)* Power Builders in *random* sequence from his or her assigned level; as soon as the student's scores show adequate progress (as discussed on pages 37–38 and 42) the student should advance to the next color level in the kit. Thus, the number of Power Builders that any student will work in a particular level will vary according to his or her abilities and learning rate and the level at which the student is working. A typical student should probably do at least six Power Builders in a level; others may do eight or ten. Only the very slowest student is likely to require practice with all fifteen Power Builders in a level before moving on. Over the course of the program, it is estimated that a typical student generally will work a total of twenty to thirty Power Builders.

After the training phase, you should begin holding **WEEKLY CONFERENCES** with each student to review his or her progress. You are strongly encouraged to make these conferences *mutual* consultations in which you and the student decide *together* whether or not it is time to move to a new level. Getting students accustomed to taking responsibility for their own learning progress is important if you are to realize the full potential of the SRA READING LABORATORY system as a builder not just of skills, but of self-image and self-confidence as well.

*While free choice of Power Builders by individuals is consistent with the Laboratory's purpose and design, the procedure described later in this Handbook eliminates individual choice so as to reduce the confusion that can attend traffic to and from the Laboratory box. Student helpers or group leaders who pass out the Student Record Books (SRBs) can insert a Power Builder into each SRB, giving each student any Power Builder that he or she has not yet read in the assigned color level. (This is revealed by the Power Builder Chart on the front of the student's SRB.) In this system, the group leaders also collect the materials at the end of the period, refile the Power Builders in the Laboratory box, and store the SRBs in a central location. Whether to use this group-leader system or let each student select his or her own materials from the box is up to each individual teacher.

Materials

The SRA READING LABORATORY kit contains the following materials:

◆ POWER BUILDERS

These are the core of the SRA READING LABORATORY program. There are 150 four-page Power Builder folders arranged in ten color-coded levels of graduated difficulty. Each **Power Builder** has four parts:

1 An illustrated, high-interest reading selection

2 "How Well Did You Read?"—a section of comprehension questions about the reading selection

3 "Learn about Words"—five exercises on vocabulary development, word analysis, and study skills

4 "Use Your Imagination"—a section that encourages creative expression through projects designed for use by individuals or groups (occasionally omitted to make room for word study exercises of unusual length)

◆ STUDENT RECORD BOOK (SRB)

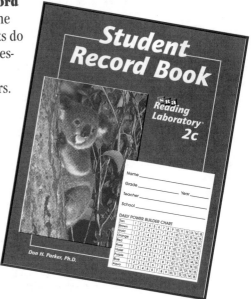

Each student receives his or her own copy of the **Student Record Book**. This is the student's personal record of work completed in the SRA READING LABORATORY program. It is the place where students do all their writing: recording their answers to the various exercise questions on special record pages; correcting their mistakes; recording their scores; and charting their progress through the Power Builders. This book serves additionally as an operating guide for the SRA READING LABORATORY program, as it contains a description of Laboratory procedures, sample pages on which trial exercises can be worked for practice, and helpful suggestions for effective reading and study habits. It also contains the Starting Level Guide, which is the placement device for starting each student in his or her individualized SRA READING LABORATORY program at the appropriate level. Five copies of the Student Record Book are supplied with each Laboratory kit; additional copies can be ordered according to need.

◆ POWER BUILDER KEY CARDS

Every Power Builder has a corresponding **Key Card** with the answers to the Power Builder questions. Students use the Key Card to score their own work. When the student's responses indicate a weakness in a comprehension skill, the Key Card directs the student to an appropriate Comprehension Strategy lesson in *Strategies for Reading and Writing*.

◆ STRATEGIES FOR READING AND WRITING

This booklet consists of two sections; the first provides Comprehension Strategy lessons for the comprehension skills listed in Appendix F, and the second gives writing strategies and prompts for each color level of the Power Builders. The writing prompts direct students to use narrative, informational, or persuasive writing to compose a variety of selections, from biographies to letters to the editor.

◆ TEACHER'S HANDBOOK

The **handbook** you are now reading contains full details of the SRA READING LABORATORY program and provides teaching plans for using the program to maximum advantage. In addition, the six separate appendixes of the References and Resources section should answer any question you are likely to have.

GETTING STARTED:
The Basic Steps of the Program

These are the basic steps for using the SRA READING LABORATORY program.

1 ADMINISTER the Starting Level Guide

Administer the Starting Level Guide to help determine the appropriate color level at which students should begin reading. The Starting Level Guide also familiarizes students with the structure of the Power Builders. *(For more information, see pages 17–20 in this guide.)*

2 INTRODUCE the Reading Laboratory

Introduce the Reading Laboratory and tell students about each component of the Laboratory kit. Then walk students through the SQR learning format. *(For more information, see pages 21–23 in this guide.)*

3 INTRODUCE the Power Builders

Introduce the Power Builders by working each section of the Power Builder Starter in the Student Record Book with students. As you work the Power Builder, show students how to record their answers on the Power Builder Record Page. *(For more information, see pages 24–26 in this guide.)*

4 INTRODUCE the Power Builder record keeping

Explain to students how to use the Conversion Table and the Progress Chart in the Student Record Book. *(For more information, see pages 27–29 in this guide.)*

5 HELP students with their first Power Builder

Review the Power Builder procedures and show students how to use the Answer Key and how to use the Power Builder Checklist in the Student Record Book to be sure they know the steps they must follow. *(For more information, see pages 30–33 in this guide.)*

6 HELP students with comprehension questions and review SQR technique

Before students do a Power Builder independently, explain the comprehension hints in the Student Record Book. Then review the SQR technique. *(For more information, see pages 34–35 in this guide.)*

7 REVIEW "Learn about Words"

Before students do another Power Builder independently, review how to complete the "Learn about Words" section of the Power Builders. *(For more information, see page 36 in this guide.)*

8 INTRODUCE study tips, conduct individual conferences, and describe Strategies for Reading and Writing

Discuss study tips with students and allow them to do Power Builders within their color level. As they work, begin individual student conferences to review students' work. Then introduce them to the Reading Comprehension Strategy lessons in the *Strategies for Reading and Writing* booklet. *(For more information, see pages 37–39 in this guide.)*

9 REVIEW Power Builders and the SQR formula

Review the SQR formula with students. Then have them complete the Power Builder Follow-up in the Student Record Book. *(For more information, see page 40 in this guide.)*

10 INTRODUCE "Use Your Imagination" and writing prompts

After students finish scoring their Power Builders, discuss the "Use Your Imagination" section at the end of the Power Builders. Then introduce the writing prompts in the *Strategies for Reading and Writing* booklet. *(For more information, see pages 41–42 in this guide.)*

11 USE SQR with textbooks

Review SQR techniques and show students how to use the SQR method with other materials, such as textbooks. Then proceed with a Power Builder session. *(For more information, see page 43 in this guide.)*

12 HELP students conduct a final analysis of their performance

Help students complete the final evaluation section on the last page of the Starting Level Guide. *(For more information, see page 44 in this guide.)*

Self-checking with the Laboratory's Answer Key cards gives students the immediate feedback on which motivation and success depend.

In periodic conferences, the teacher and the student review the Progress Charts together and reach a joint decision on whether it's time to move ahead to a more difficult color level.

Recommended Schedule and Teaching Plans

◆ We include here a schedule and teaching plans for introducing the components of your SRA READING LABORATORY kit and monitoring students' progress. The schedule covers a training phase and an independent phase for using the Power Builders. For reasons detailed on page 9, it is considered best to schedule the Power Builder sessions close together. Unless otherwise noted, each day's session is assumed to be thirty to forty-five minutes long.

For ease of instruction, certain passages in the teaching plans are "scripted" so that you can read them aloud directly to the class if you wish (or paraphrase them if you prefer). Such passages are signaled by shading behind the text. The remaining passages are for your information and are not meant to be read aloud.

These teaching plans are fully detailed through the first eleven sessions. After that, specific procedures are given only for the Final Analysis. By then, the normal Laboratory procedures will have become routine, and students will be working independently.

The time of your heaviest involvement in the SRA READING LABORATORY program will be the first ten sessions—the introductory training phase during which you will establish students' starting levels, present the Power Builder program to them, and give them opportunities to practice the basic Laboratory procedures.

During the remainder of the program, students will be working independently, for the most part. Your role will be primarily that of a manager/consultant who sets the times for SRA READING LABORATORY sessions and holds conferences with individual students to review their progress and help them decide whether they are ready to move to a new level.

RECOMMENDED TEACHING SCHEDULE

Training Phase

SESSION 1	SESSION 2	SESSION 3	SESSION 4	SESSION 5
Placement of Students: Starting Level Guide *Page 17*	Introduction of Reading Laboratory Components: SQR Formula *Page 21*	Learning Power Builder Procedures (Power Builder Starter) *Page 24*	Power Builder Record-Keeping Procedures (Conversion Table, Progress Chart) *Page 27*	Power Builders (Students Work Their First Power Builder Independently) *Page 30*

SESSION 6	SESSION 7	SESSION 8	SESSION 9	SESSION 10
Power Builders (Comprehension and SQR Review) *Page 34*	Power Builders (Review "Learn about Words") *Page 36*	Study Tips, Power Builders, and Individual Conferences, Reading Comprehension Strategy Lessons *Page 37*	Power Builders (Review of Procedures), SQR Review *Page 40*	Power Builders ("Use Your Imagination" Introduced), Writing Prompts *Page 41*

Independent Phase

Review the SQR technique with students and show them how to apply it to their work with textbooks. Follow this with a regular Power Builder session. (See page 43.) After this session, conduct more Power Builder sessions, spaced close together, and end the program with a final analysis. (See page 44.)

Summary Today, you will administer the Starting Level Guide, found at the beginning of the Student Record Book (pages 4–7). It is the device for determining the color level at which each student should enter the Power Builder program. The Starting Level Guide also gives students a first taste of what it is like to read a Power Builder story and answer the associated questions.

PROCEDURES

Take a look at the Starting Level Guide (called SLG hereafter) before class. It begins with seven questions, followed by three stories (one of which is an example). When you administer the SLG, make sure that you allow enough time for students to complete all three stories during the same class session; otherwise, the results will not be accurate.

Write the following on the chalkboard, filling in the Grade, Year, Teacher, and School blanks as appropriate.

Name _____ **Teacher** _____

Grade _____ **Year** _____ **School** _____

Pass out the Student Record Books. Say:

> ◆ **I AM** passing out the Student Record Books for the SRA READING LABORATORY kit. This will be your very own book, in which you will keep track of your work in the Laboratory. When you receive it, write your name on the front cover after the word *Name*. Also fill in the Teacher, Grade, Year, and School lines just as you see them on the chalkboard. Leave these booklets on your desks unopened for the time being. Do *not* open them yet.
>
> Some of you have worked with SRA READING LABORATORY kits before. If so, this one will be familiar to you.
>
> By finding out today how well each of you reads, we'll decide the best place for each of you to start building better reading skills. How do we do this? We use something called a Starting Level Guide. It's at the beginning of your Student Record Book on page 4. Open your books now and let's look at that page together.
>
> At the top of page 4, write the same information that you wrote on the cover of your books. Do that now.

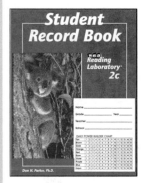

Student Record Book (SRB)

Next, go over the seven questions on page 4 one at a time to make sure students understand them. Then, have students answer the questions in the spaces provided. Do not let them discuss their responses with each other. When they have finished writing, say:

> ◆ **LOOK** at the bottom part of page 4. Find the word **Example** in heavy type. Below that word is a short paragraph, or story. To the left of that word are some directions. Read those directions silently while I read them aloud.

Read the directions and let students ask questions. Then, say:

> ◆ **REMEMBER** to write your answer in the box at the right-hand side of the page. For example, the answer to question 1 of the example story is **a, b, c,** or **d.** So you will choose the letter you think is correct and write that letter in the first box. If you want to change your answer, *don't erase.* Just make an X through it and write your corrections beside it, like this.

Draw on chalkboard.

Demonstrate on the chalkboard how a correction should be made. Make sure students understand the procedures. Next, say:

> ◆ **READY?** Now, read the example story and answer both of the questions.

Allow about one minute for everyone to finish. Then, say:

> ◆ **STOP!** Put your pencils down. Now, we will see how well you understood what you just read.

Read aloud the first comprehension question. Then, call on a student to give his or her response to it. Ask the student to say not only the letter written, but also the words that go with it: for example, **c, walk on its tail on command.** Before giving the correct response, ask whether other students have given different answers. If so, guide them to reread that part of the paragraph where the right answer is to be found. Confirm that **c** is the right answer, and proceed in the same way with the second comprehension question, to which the correct answer is **b, on top of the water.** When you are sure that all students understand the mechanics, say:

◆ **NEXT,** you will read two more stories followed by questions. These stories will be a little longer and will be followed by more questions. When I give the signal—don't start yet—you will turn the page and find Story A. You will fold your books back like this so that only Story A can be seen. *(Demonstrate.)*

Then, you will have three minutes to read the entire story at the top of the page and to read and answer the five questions under it. You may look back at the story. If you make a mistake, remember not to erase but to correct it as I showed you on the chalkboard. Read as rapidly as you can without losing the meaning of what you are reading. When you've answered all the questions, stop. Ready? Turn the page and fold the book so you can only see Story A on page 5. . . . Start reading.

Look at your watch immediately. Exact timing is very important on Stories A and B. When exactly three minutes have passed, say:

◆ **STOP** working. Now, we are going to do the other story, Story B. When I give the signal—do not start yet—you will simply open your books out flat so that you can see Story B on the right-hand side. This story is a little longer, and it has eight questions. Some of you may not finish reading it and answering all the questions before I call time, but that's all right. Just do as much as you can. Read rapidly, but not so fast that you miss the meaning. When you come to the bottom of the page, turn to the next page, where there are three more questions. Ready? Open your books out flat. . . . Begin reading Story B.

Exactly three minutes later, say:

◆ **STOP** working. Pass in your Student Record Books.

To correct the SLGs, use the key on the inside front cover of this Handbook. Each student's SLG score is the sum of his or her correct answers to Story A and Story B. Use the placement chart given here to determine each student's starting level for the Power Builder program.

2c Placement Chart

Find the student's SLG score in the top row. Start the student in the color level indicated below that score (middle row for students in the first half of grade 6; bottom row for students in the second half of grade 6).

Student's SLG Score	3 or below	4	5	6	7	8	9	10 or above
Starting Placement (first half of grade 6)	Aqua	Aqua	Blue	Purple	Violet	Violet	Rose	Red
Starting Placement (second half of grade 6)	Aqua	Aqua	Blue	Purple	Violet	Rose	Red	Orange

The color levels on the chart correspond to approximate reading-grade levels as follows:

Aqua	3.0	Rose	5.0
Blue	3.5	Red	5.5
Purple	4.0	Orange	6.0
Violet	4.5		

Daily Power Builder Chart

Tan	1	2	3	4	5	6	7	8
Brown	1	2	3	4	5	6	7	8
Gold	1	2	3	4	5	6	7	8
Orange	1	2	3	4	5	6	7	8
Red	1	2	3	4	5	6	7	8
Rose	1	2	3	4	5	6	7	8
Violet	1	2	3	4	5	6	7	8
Purple	1	2	3	4	5	6	7	8
Blue	1	2	3	4	5	6	7	8
Aqua	1	2	3	4	5	6	7	8

From SRB, front cover

After determining each student's starting level, turn to the cover of his or her Student Record Book and circle the color name on the Power Builder Chart. The sample chart shown here indicates that this student will begin work in the Power Builder program at the Purple level.

You may either remove the Starting Level Guides from the SRBs and store them in a safe place, or simply leave them in students' SRBs. You will be asking students to refer to them again in the Final Analysis session.

Introduction of Reading Laboratory Components; SQR Formula

Summary Today, you will introduce the concept of the multilevel learning program, acquaint your students with the various components of the Laboratory kit, and teach them the "Survey-Question-Read" (SQR) technique for effective study.

PROCEDURES

Talk with students about the results of the Starting Level Guides they completed yesterday. Explain that it turned out that there are various reading levels in the class. Then, present the components of the SRA READING LABORATORY program to them. Begin by holding up a Power Builder folder. Say:

◆ **THERE** are 150 of these Power Builders. Each one begins with an interesting story on pages 1 and 2, and that story is followed by some questions on pages 3 and 4. These Power Builders are in ten groups, each group having its own special color. One of these colors will be just right for you as you start out—not too easy, and not too hard. When you have material that is just right for you, you learn to read more easily. I'll tell each of you what color you should start with, based on the results of yesterday's work with the Starting Level Guide. That color level is where you'll begin the program. In time, as you improve your skills, you will move to other colors.

The Clever Wizard
Told by Mesfin Habte-Mariam

Power Builder

Hold up a Student Record Book opened to a Power Builder Record Page (any page from 25 through 61).

◆ **THIS** is a Power Builder Record Page. There are a number of pages like this in your Student Record Book. This is where you will write all your answers to the questions in the Power Builders. You must never write on a Power Builder because other students will use it after you.

Power Builder Record Page
(from SRB)

Hold up a Power Builder Key Card.

◆ **THIS** is a Power Builder Key Card. It has the answers to the questions on one of the Power Builders. There is a Key Card like this for every Power Builder. The Key Card tells you when your answers are right and when they are not. If you find that you've made a mistake, you should always look back at the Power Builder to find out where you went wrong. If you make mistakes in comprehension skills, you go to a Reading Comprehension Strategy lesson in the Strategies for Reading and Writing booklet. Now, I have only two more things to show you—but they are very important.

Pass out the Student Record Books—each to the student whose name is on the cover.

◆ **THIS** is the Student Record Book that you used yesterday when you worked the Starting Level Guide. All of your written answers will go in this book—never on any of the Power Builders from the Laboratory kit. Your Student Record Book also contains information about the Power Builders, and we will read some of this information together. Also, on the cover, I have circled the name of the color level in which each of you will begin your work with the Power Builders.

Invite students to explore their Student Record Books briefly. Then, tell them to close their books. On the chalkboard, write the word *Survey*, using an oversized S. Explain that this word means "to look over," and that they have just been surveying their Student Record Books.

Ask students if any questions occurred to them as they surveyed. When some have responded, write the word *Question* (oversized *Q*) under the word *Survey*. Under the word *Question*, write the word *Read* (oversized *R*). Then, say:

Survey

Question

Read

Write on chalkboard.

◆ **HERE** you have a formula that will help you read and study better: SQR. First, you Survey, then you Question, and then you are ready to Read—and to understand what you read. You will learn to use this formula with the Power Builders of the SRA READING LABORATORY program. Later, you can use SQR to help you with all your studying, including the study of textbooks. Now, open your Student Record Books to page 8.

Read aloud the section titled "Survey," or ask a volunteer to do so. Ask the class to look at the story on pages 9 and 10 and to survey the elements listed: the picture, the title, the first and last paragraphs. Then ask various students to tell what they saw when they surveyed the story. Point again to the words *Survey*, *Question*, and *Read* on the chalkboard. Say:

> ◆ **TRY** to remember SQR—Survey, Question, and Read. Tomorrow we will read the story, and you'll begin to see how the SQR formula helps you read and understand better.

At the close of this class and those that follow, Student Record Books should be collected and returned to a designated place.

Learning Power Builder Procedures (Power Builder Starter)

Summary   Pages 9 through 12 of the Student Record Book contain a sample Power Builder (known as the "Power Builder Starter") for use in acquainting students with the Power Builder procedures that apply at every level. Today, you and your students will work this sample selection together.

P R O C E D U R E S

Distribute the SRBs. Ask students to open to page 8 and read again the "Survey" section. Then, read aloud the "Question" and "Read" sections. Next, say:

SRB, page 9

> ◆ **ORDINARILY** you will read the Power Builder stories to your-selves, but today I'm going to read a sample story to you. Look at the story that starts on page 9. It's just like the Power Builder folders I showed you from the Laboratory box. As I read, look at the story and follow along silently.

When you have finished reading, ask students to look at page 13, the first of their Power Builder Record Pages. Say:

> ◆ **YOU** will always write your answers on pages like this one. Never write on a Power Builder.
>
> Now, at the top of the left-hand column of this page, write today's date in the space after "Date." Skip the space after "Color" and come down to the line where it says "Power Builder Number." On that line, write the letter *S* for Starter.
>
> Put your finger where it says "How Well Did You Read?" Following the story in the Power Builder Starter, there are some ques-tions that have this same title. This is where you will write your answers to those questions. Let's look at those questions now. Turn back to page 11.

SRB, page 13

Read aloud the directions for "How Well Did You Read?" on page 11. Then, read comprehension question 1. Ask a student to give a response. If other students do not agree, invite them to look back at the story and read the part that supports the answer they chose. Tell students that looking back is always permitted, as it can help them think through a question. Then, ask them to return to the Record Page (13) and write the correct letter (b) after the number 1. Remind students that when they record their answers they should never make erasures. To change an answer, they should simply draw an X through it and write their new answer alongside.

When you are sure everyone knows how to proceed, let each student read silently and respond to the remaining five comprehension questions. When they have finished, write the correct responses on the chalkboard (1–b; 2–a; 3–c; 4–b; 5–c; 6–b). Then, say:

SRB, page 11

> ◆ **IF** your answers are the same as these, leave them just as they are. If you have a different answer, it is incorrect. To show that it is wrong, draw a circle around it and write the correct letter beside it like this.

Use the chalkboard to demonstrate once again this method of marking a mistake.

Ask the class to turn back to page 11 and find the "Learn about Words" section. Read aloud the introduction and instructions in Section A. Let the students turn back to the paragraph referenced in the first question (paragraph 1) and find the word that best fits the meaning of "with honor." Have them write the correct answer (proudly) on the Record Page. Then let each student read silently and respond to the remaining six items in section A. Allow enough time for a majority of the students to complete the work.

Write the correct answers for section A on the chalkboard (1–proudly; 2–ideals; 3–suit; 4–design; 5–Enlightening; 6–moisture; 7–pedestal). Have students correct their work as before. Then, let them finish the rest of the thirty-three "Learn about Words" items.

Ask the class to turn to the key for the Power Builder Starter (SRB, page 62). Let them use this answer key to check their answers to the questions in sections B, C, D, and E.

SRB, page 62

Make sure that students take time to learn from their mistakes. Whenever they make a mistake, they should take time to refer back to the Power Builder story, see why they responded as they did, and reflect on why another response is better. This immediate-feedback procedure is far more beneficial than merely accepting the verdict of the Key Card and moving on. Comprehension skills will be strengthened if students will perform this review for every mistake.

When all students have finished, ask them to look at the lower half of the right-hand column of the Record Page, evaluate their work, and decide how they could do better next time. Then, say:

> ◆ **THAT** is all we're going to do today. Tomorrow you will learn how to score your work and mark your Power Builder Progress Chart.

Collect the SRBs and file them in a convenient place. Do not be discouraged if not all students complete the work in this, their first Power Builder experience. Later, you will have time to help slower students master the procedures. If a number of students have difficulty with this session, you can form a small group apart from the rest of the class and go over the Power Builder Starter with them after this session.

Summary Today, you will show students the procedures for using their SRBs to keep an accurate record of their work. This entails using the **Conversion Table** (inside back cover of SRB) to determine the percentage score and posting this information on the Power Builder Progress Chart.

PROCEDURES

Choose several group leaders, one for every five or six students. Each group leader will distribute the SRBs to students of his or her row or table. When this is done, say:

◆ **YESTERDAY** you learned how to read a Power Builder and do the exercises. You also learned to record your answers on a Record Page. Now, turn to page 14 in your Student Record Books. You'll find that the blanks have already been filled in.

Put your finger on the heading "How Well Did You Read?" Look at the blanks under it. How many are there? . . . Yes, there are ten. Some Power Builders have as many as ten comprehension questions; others have only five. How many comprehension questions were there in the Power Builder that this student did? . . . Yes, there were six.

Now, look just below the "How Well Did You Read?" blanks, where it says "Possible right." Since there were six comprehension questions on the Power Builder, it was possible to get six right. So this student wrote 6 in the blank after "Possible right."

Now, look at the circled letters. They are the student's wrong answers. Of the six possible right answers, how many did the student get right? . . . Yes, four. Look just below "Possible right," where it says "Number right." The student wrote 4 in the blank because four was the actual number this student got right.

Now, look at the blank after "Percentage right." The student has written 67 to show that four right answers is 67 percent of a possible six. How did the student know that? You'll find out if you turn to the inside back cover of your Student Record Book and the page that faces the cover. Turn back there now, and we'll study these pages together.

SRB, page 14

Read aloud paragraph 1 under "How to Use Your Progress Charts" at the top of page 63. When you read about a certain part of the Conversion Table, ask students to put a finger on it. This will help to focus their attention on each step.

> ◆ **NOW,** you are going to calculate your own percentage right. Turn back to the Power Builder Record Page you filled in yesterday— page 13. You wrote answers to six comprehension questions, so the number of "possible rights" is six. Write 6 in the blank after "Possible right." Now, count your right answers and write that number in the blank after "Number right."

Have each student do the same with his or her answers for "Learn about Words," entering 33 after "Possible right" and his or her own score after "Number right." Then, have students determine their percentages, using the Conversion Table on the inside back cover of their books. Tell them to enter those percentages on the Power Builder Record Page.

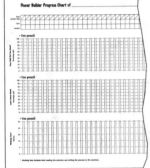

From SRB, inside back cover

Ask students to fold out the back cover of their books so that they can see the Power Builder Progress Chart. Have them enter their names at the top of the chart. Then, have them enter the date at the top of the first column. In the first space, following the word *Number,* have them write *S* for *Starter.* Have them leave the space blank after the word *Color.*

Read aloud paragraphs 2 and 3 on page 63. Then, on the chalkboard, draw a rough sketch of the "How Well Did You Read?" section of the Progress Chart as illustrated here.

Ask one student what percentage he or she achieved on "How Well Did You Read?" Draw a heavy dot at that point on your chalkboard sketch. Then, erase it and draw a dot to show the percentage of another student. Do this several times until all understand. Then, say:

> ◆ **USE** your pencil to put a black dot on your Progress Chart for "How Well Did You Read?"

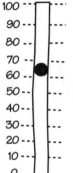

Draw on chalkboard.

While students are doing this, walk around the class and look at the charts. Offer help as needed. Tell students to mark their percentages right on the "Learn about Words" chart as well. Again, check the charts.

Return to your chalkboard sketch now and draw a heavy dot to show 67 percent. Then, fill in the column from zero up to the dot. Ask students to use their pencils to make a similar dot on their progress charts at the appropriate point (their individual "percentage right" figures) and fill in the column up to that dot. This completes the marking of their Progress Charts.

Have group leaders collect the SRBs and return them to the designated storage area.

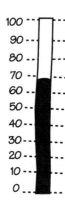

Draw on chalkboard.

Summary   Today, each student will work with an actual Power Builder from the Laboratory box at his or her own level. First, however, you will review Power Builder procedures with students and show them how to use the Power Builder Checklist (inside back cover of SRB) as a convenient reminder of the steps they must follow.

Note: In general, allow approximately thirty to forty-five minutes for each session of the SRA READING LABORATORY program. Because of individual differences, students will work at different speeds. Early in the program, slower students may require more than one period to complete a Power Builder, but later on many students will have some time left over at the end of the period. Such a student should not go on to begin another Power Builder in that remaining time, however, for if Power Builder work is hurried, the student's work may degenerate into a pointless race with time. Instead, such a student should be given a change of pace—a chance to read library books or other materials for pleasure, for example.

PROCEDURES

Before the class begins, choose a Power Builder for each student to read from the color level you circled on the student's Power Builder Chart.

If the color is, say, Aqua, select any Power Builder from the Aqua level; the student need not work the Power Builders from that level in any particular order.

Insert the Power Builder into the student's SRB so that the number and color of the Power Builder protrude and are visible. After this first time, you can instruct your group leaders in performing this task. Today, have them distribute the SRBs with the Power Builders already inserted by you. Say:

Power Builder Checklist

Power Builder Checklist

This list will serve as a guide when you do your first few Power Builders. Simply make a check after each step as you do it. When you have done some Power Builders, you won't need this list. You will remember to do each step at the right time.

Where?	Do what?	Done?
This Book	1 Fill in Power Builder Chart.	
Record Page	2 Record date, color, and number.	
	3 Record starting time.	
Power Builder	4 Read selection.	
	5 Do "How Well Did You Read?"	
	6 Do "Learn about Words."	
Record Page	7 Record finishing time and figure working time.	
	8 Get key and score work.	
	9 Record number right.	
This Book	10 Use table to find percentage right.	
Record Page	11 Record percentage right.	
This Book	12 Color graph on progress chart.	
	13 Graph working time.	
Record Page	14 Evaluate work.	

From SRB, inside back cover

◆ **WHEN** you receive your Student Record Book, don't remove the Power Builder from it. Simply turn the book face down and open the back cover. On the inside of the back cover, find the section headed "Power Builder Checklist." It is below the Conversion Table that you used yesterday to determine your percentages.

So far, you have been learning how to work with Power Builders, using the samples in your Student Record Book. Now, you will begin to work with the real Power Builders from the Laboratory box. This

Power Builder Checklist will help you remember to do all the steps in the right order.

1 Fill in Power Builder Chart.

From SRB, inside back cover

Read step 1. Then, ask students to look at the Power Builder Chart on the front of the SRB and note the color that has been circled. Then, say:

◆ **THIS** is the color in which you will start your Power Builder work. It is the color that was indicated by the Starting Level Guide that you took a few days ago. Don't take out the Power Builder yet, but do look at the color block with the number. It is on the edge of your Power Builder. It must always be the color that is marked on your Power Builder Chart.

Look at the number of your Power Builder. Now, on the Power Builder Chart, look at the row of numbers following your circled color. Run your finger along that row until you find the number of the Power Builder you were given. Take your pencil and darken that box. You will do this each time you receive a new Power Builder. Then, your chart will always show which Power Builders you've already received, and you won't be given the same one twice.

But suppose you don't finish your Power Builder by the end of class. In that case, you will want to get it back again. If so, just erase the darkening-in, and make an X in the box instead. That will tell the group leader to give the Power Builder back to you. You can read the Power Builders in any order; you may read number 15 first and number 1 last. But you must work in the same color until your scores show that you have mastered the skills of that level. Almost always, you will need to do at least six Power Builders before going on to the next level. You may also need to do some Reading Comprehension Strategy lessons if you missed any of the answers in "How Well Did You Read?" that are marked with a star on the Key Card.

Daily Power Builder Chart

Tan	1	2	3	4	5	6	7	8
Brown	1	2	3	4	5	6	7	8
Gold	1	2	3	4	5	6	7	8
Orange	1	2	3	4	5	6	7	8
Red	1	2	3	4	5	6	7	8
Rose	1	2	3	4	5	6	7	8
Violet	1	2	3	4	5	6	7	8
Purple	1	2	3	4	5	■	7	8
Blue	1	2	3	4	5	6	7	8
Aqua	1	2	3	4	5	6	7	8

From SRB, front cover

Daily Power Builder Chart

Tan	1	2	3	4	5	6	7	8
Brown	1	2	3	4	5	6	7	8
Gold	1	2	3	4	5	6	7	8
Orange	1	2	3	4	5	6	7	8
Red	1	2	3	4	5	6	7	8
Rose	1	2	3	4	5	6	7	8
Violet	1	2	3	4	5	6	7	8
Purple	1	2	3	4	5	X	7	8
Blue	1	2	3	4	5	6	7	8
Aqua	1	2	3	4	5	6	7	8

From SRB, front cover

● ●

Date (month/day) *Sept. 18*

Power Builder color *Purple*

Power Builder number *12*

Finishing time *10:55*

Starting time *10:15*

Working time *40*

From SRB, page 14

---

2 Record date, color, and number.
3 Record starting time.

---

4 Read selection.
5 Do "How Well Did You Read?"
6 Do "Learn about Words."

---

7 Record finishing time
    and figure working time.

---

8 Get key and score work.

From SRB, inside back cover

Ask students to turn back to the Checklist. Read steps 2 and 3.

Now, have students turn to the Sample Power Builder Record Page (SRB, page 14).

◆ **LOOK** at the top left-hand part of this page. The student has filled in the date, the color, and the number.

Look down the column to where it says, "Starting time." The student has written 10:15, the time he or she began to do the Power Builder work. There are also some other times written there. We'll look at those in a minute.

Turn back to the Checklist for steps 4, 5, and 6. (Read these steps aloud.) You know these steps because you did them yesterday. You read the selection and did both sets of exercises.

Step 7 is "Record finishing time and working time." Look back at the Sample Record Page, page 14. The student has written 10:55 in the blank after "Finishing time." That is the time he or she finished reading the story and completing the exercises. The student figured the working time by subtracting the starting time from the finishing time. You will figure your working time for each Power Builder you do.

Step 8 on the Checklist is "Get key and score work." You scored your work yesterday, using keys that were on the chalkboard and in your books. But when you work with the actual Power Builders from the Laboratory box, you will correct your work with Key Cards that also come from the box.

Hold up a Power Builder and the Key Card that goes with it from the Laboratory box.

> ◆ **EACH** Power Builder has its own Power Builder Key Card. The Key Card has the same color and the same number as the Power Builder. When you finish your Power Builder, go to the Laboratory box and take out the Key Card that goes with your Power Builder. Take that Key Card to your desk and correct your work. Your group leader will collect the Key Card along with the Power Builder and your Student Record Book at the end of the session.
>
> Steps 9, 10, 11, and 12 are also familiar to you from yesterday's work. You recorded your number right, used the Conversion Table to find your percentage right, recorded that, and marked your Progress Chart.

9	Record number right.
10	Use table to find percentage right.
11	Record percentage right.
12	Color graph on progress chart.

Ask students to turn to page 63 of their SRBs. Read paragraph 4 and call attention to the illustration.

Read paragraph 5 from SRB page 63 and call attention to the illustration.

> ◆ **GRAPHING** your working time is step 13. You must always use a black pencil for this. On all your graphs, you also use a black pencil to join the black dots.
>
> The last step on the Checklist is "Evaluate work." You did this after you worked the Power Builder Starter; you rated your work as poor, fair, good, or excellent, and you told how you could do better next time.
>
> Now that you know every step of the Power Builder Checklist, you are ready to start work with your Power Builder. As you do each step, make a check in the box on the Checklist. When you have done several Power Builders, you won't need to refer to the Checklist anymore. You will remember what to do without it.

13	Graph working time.

14	Evaluate work.

From SRB, inside back cover

Tell students that for now they can ignore "Use Your Imagination" at the end of the Power Builder. This feature, which encourages written and oral creativity and self-expression, will be dealt with later. Tell students they may begin their Power Builders.

Power Builders
(Comprehension and SQR Review)

Summary Today, you will pass on some useful hints about answering comprehension questions, and you will review the SQR technique with students prior to having them work a Power Builder on their own. Their work cannot be entirely independent at this stage, however. Be prepared to answer a number of questions and to assist with procedures, as students are likely to experience considerable uncertainty during these early sessions.

The most important thing about answering questions and giving help is to do it promptly, at the moment of need. Students can then quickly move ahead on their own. A major advantage of the SRA READING LABORATORY'S learner-operated system is that it frees the teacher to give prompt help when it's needed.

PROCEDURES

Have group leaders pass out the SRBs with a Power Builder inserted. Ask students to turn to page 16 and look at the section headed "Hints about Comprehension Checks." Read the introductory paragraph and hint 1. Then, ask:

> ◆ **SUPPOSE** you saw the question "What was the main idea?" What would you look for in the story in order to choose the right answer? Suppose you were asked to find the problem in the story. What would you look for?

Read hint 2. Write the following examples on the chalkboard and let students choose the best answer for each.

The sun's rays can

  a make plants grow

  b burn people's skin

  c Both **a** and **b**

A dog can learn to
  a beg for food
  b read a book
  c Both **a** and **b**

Read hint 3. Again, write these examples on the chalkboard and let the students choose the best answer.

Work is
  a always fun
  b sometimes fun
  c never fun

Angry animals
  a bite
  b growl
  c Both **a** and **b**

Remind students that sometimes they will need to read a comprehension question more than once to understand it fully.

Before students begin working with their Power Builders, conduct a brief review of the SQR technique (SRB, page 8). Ask students to name the three steps (Survey, Question, Read) and write these on the chalkboard as they do so. Ask for, and list under Survey, the four places the eyes should go in the Survey step (picture, title, first paragraph, and last paragraph).

Remind students to use the Power Builder Checklist (inside back cover of SRB) in order to be sure of performing all the steps in the right order.

Tell students to raise their hands whenever they have a question about what to do next. Then, let them begin their Power Builders.

Survey
  picture
  title
  first paragraph
  last paragraph
Question
Read

Write on chalkboard.

SESSION 7

Power Builders
(Review "Learn about Words")

Summary Today, you will go over the section How "Learn about Words" Works before having students work another Power Builder. Continue during this session and those that follow to give students individual help—procedural and otherwise—whenever they need it.

Have the group leaders distribute the SRBs with Power Builders inside. Ask the class to turn to page 16 and look at the section How "Learn about Words" Works. Read the section aloud and answer any questions students may have.

Let students proceed to work their Power Builders. Remind them to refer to the Power Builder Checklist, to use the SQR technique, and to ask for help whenever they need it.

Summary   Today, you will introduce the section "When You Study" (SRB, page 15) and review the work that individual students have been doing. One of the first things you want to find out is whether the student has been correctly placed in the SRA READING LABORATORY'S programs. The Starting Level Guide that you administered earlier is not a precise instrument, although it is a good general indicator of the probable best level at which a student should begin Laboratory work. Psychological factors, some uneasiness about working under pressure of time, or simply lucky guessing may result in a student's scoring lower or higher on the SLG than actual ability warrants. If this was the case, it should become apparent now as you review the student's progress charts, and an adjustment of the student's placement can be made.

In conference, you will want to evaluate the student's attitude and adjustment to independent work as well as his or her performance scores.

PROCEDURES

Have the group leaders distribute the SRBs. Tell students to turn to page 15 and read the "When You Study" questionnaire. Instruct them to think about each question honestly and mark an X in the box that indicates their own habits most accurately.

When students have completed the page, you may either ask them to work Power Builders or allow them a free-reading period.

While the class is working, begin your conferences with individual students. Ask a student to come to your desk, bringing along his or her SRB.

Note the student's percentage scores and working time. If the scores are consistently low—below 70 percent—or if the student is working very slowly, let him or her drop back a color level or two. If the student has consistently high scores within normal working times, you may want to let the student move to a higher level. But if students are unable to handle even the easiest level in the *Reading Laboratory 2c* kit, you should consider putting them in the 2b or 2a kit.

Once a student has been correctly placed in a color level, you need only check his or her progress charts to see when the student is ready to move to another level. If students miss any of the starred answers on the Key Card in the "How Well Did

From SRB, page 15

You Read?" section, direct them to the appropriate Reading Comprehension Strategy lesson in the *Strategies for Reading and Writing* booklet. Guidelines for determining when a student is ready to move are given after Session 10 (page 42).

You will want to evaluate the student's adjustment to independent work as well as his or her performance. Is the student comfortable with the responsibility that the SRA READING LABORATORY system places on him or her to take charge of his or her own learning program? Is the student conscientiously trying to learn from mistakes by going back to the story and its questions to see why errors were made? Or is he or she just mechanically going through the steps of marking answers right and wrong? Has the student asked for a lot of help, even though capable of doing the work? No student should need continuous assistance if placed at his or her optimum working level in the program. Because the SRA READING LABORATORY system enables the instructor to give students a great deal of personal attention, some students may take advantage of this fact. If so, you should point out that each student is responsible for his or her own progress. You are there to help, but in the end it is the student who must take charge of his or her own learning and make progress happen.

If you are comfortable with the peer-assistance concept, you may find it useful to invoke this practice at this time. Students who quickly grasp the details of the program can be very helpful in explaining those details to students who are still struggling with the mechanics of Laboratory work.

READING COMPREHENSION STRATEGY LESSONS

◆ If a student is having difficulty with a comprehension skill in the "How Well Did You Read?" section of the Power Builders, he or she will find Reading Comprehension Strategy lessons on pages 6–37 of the *Strategies for Reading and Writing* booklet. The Power Builder Key Card will direct the student to the appropriate Comprehension Strategy lesson, called Reading Strategy lesson in the book. The lesson will provide general strategies for practice in using the skill. For example, if a student is working on a Power Builder that stresses sequence, the Key Card will direct him or her to a lesson that gives tips for determining sequence and then provides a short selection and questions illustrating the use of sequence, thus walking the student through the skill. The correct answers will be printed at the back of the book. The lesson also directs students to other Power Builders that emphasize the same skill.

Hold up a *Strategies for Reading and Writing* booklet. Explain to students that the Reading Strategy lessons in the booklet will help them practice comprehension skills that they are having difficulty with. Distribute a Power Builder Key Card (any Key Card from any level) to each student. Point out the words that direct them to pages in the *Strategies for Reading and Writing* booklet. Make certain they understand that they must complete the scoring of their work with the Power Builder Key Card first, then go to the booklet and work the Reading Strategy lesson referenced on the card. As an example, pick up any Power Builder Key Card and say:

◆ **LET'S** pretend that this is the Key Card for a Power Builder I have done, and that I have missed some questions marked with a star, and the Key Card tells me to go to pages 10–13 in the *Strategies for Reading and Writing* booklet.

Hold up a *Strategies for Reading and Writing* booklet opened to page 10 and say:

◆ **ON** page 10, I read the strategies to determine the skill; and on page 11, I read the story and answer the questions illustrating the use of the skill. I write my answers on a separate sheet of paper. Then I check my answers at the back of the booklet. I can look at page 12 to see how the strategies are used in the selection, and page 13 shows me other Power Builders in my color level that deal with the same skill.

Summary Today's session is a review of the instructions and procedures for every part of a Power Builder as well as a review of the SQR formula. "More about SQR" (SRB, page 18) and the "Power Builder Follow-up" (SRB, pages 19–22) are the principal tools for this session.

When the group leaders have distributed the SRBs, ask students to turn to page 18. Read and discuss with them the sections "More about SQR" and "Skimming."

Next, have them look at the story that begins on page 19. This is the Power Builder Follow-up, a somewhat harder selection than the Power Builder Starter that the class completed in Session 3. If you think it may be too difficult for some class members, you may wish to read it aloud, as you did with the Power Builder Starter, and then have students reread it by themselves.

Students should complete the "How Well Did You Read?" and "Learn about Words" exercises on their own. They should score their own work with the Power Builder Follow-up Key (SRB, page 62) and chart their percentage right on their Power Builder Progress Chart.

Summary   Today is a regular Power Builder session. You may want to introduce students to the "Use Your Imagination" ideas at the end of most Power Builders.

PROCEDURES

When your students have finished scoring and charting their Power Builder work, call their attention to the "Use Your Imagination" paragraph at the end of most Power Builders.

These are suggestions designed to stir students' imaginations and encourage them to produce a written report or an oral presentation that can be shared with the class. Some of the suggestions call for self-expression, some for imaginative creativity, and some for research efforts.

Since students who are asked to write often find that their greatest difficulty lies in selecting a subject, the "Use Your Imagination" suggestions are uniquely valuable. They provide creative takeoff points that are always based on a story or informative article that the student has just read. Thus, the student is never being asked to write "in a vacuum," but always to write something as an extension and consequence of a stimulus just received.

Much can be accomplished with students' creative output once it has been completed. Students can exchange papers and enjoy each other's writing. They can come together in small groups to discuss, dramatize, or role-play each other's writing.

You can decide how much use you wish to make of these suggestions—whether to formalize a "Use Your Imagination" program and set aside time especially for it; to integrate these suggestions into whatever writing program you have already set up, letting them serve as additional stimuli; or simply to encourage students to respond to these suggestions independently when they feel "inspired" to do so. (Only the most highly motivated and creatively gifted children will undertake writing projects on their own without some specifically motivating occasion, so the more guidance and formal structure you provide, the more benefit can be derived from these suggestions.)

41

WRITING PROMPTS

◆ To provide further opportunity for students to practice their writing, have them turn to pages 38–59 in their *Strategies for Reading and Writing* booklet. There they will find Writing Strategy lessons that provide general tips for writing, and writing prompts for each color level that will direct them to compose a variety of selections using narrative, informational, and persuasive writing. You may want to assign a writing prompt to help engage or encourage a student who is having difficulty, or to further a successful student's motivation as he or she completes a new color level. Assignment of writing prompts should be used at your discretion to meet the needs of your students. The Writing Strategy lessons work best when appropriately assigned to individual students, rather than as a whole-class activity.

ADVANCING TO A HIGHER COLOR LEVEL

◆ After Power Builder Session 10 is over, it is time for you to help students evaluate their progress in the Power Builder program and consider whether some of them are ready to move to a higher color level. During the program, some students can be expected to advance three, four, or even five color levels.

At this stage of the program, a typical student should do at least six Power Builders and achieve scores of 85 to 100 percent in both the "How Well Did You Read?" and the "Learn about Words" sections before moving to a higher color level. The slowest students may need to do all fifteen Power Builders before they move to a new color level.

Summary Today, you will review the SQR techniques and show students how to extend it to their work with textbooks. This is followed by a regular Power Builder session.

PROCEDURES

Have the group leaders pass out the SRBs with a Power Builder inserted in each. Before having students begin work with the Power Builders, ask them to turn to page 24 in their books.

Go over with students the section entitled "Using SQR with Your Textbooks." Then, have students survey a typical assignment in one of their texts. Let two or three students perform the S and Q (Survey and Question) steps aloud using the same textbook chapter so that the class can see the flexibility of the approach; for instance, not every student will pose the same questions.

Read with the class the paragraph titled "Reading with a Purpose." Discuss the manner in which they might read a mystery story, instructions for making something, or a retailer's catalog.

Proceed with a regular Power Builder session, including scoring and posting of Progress Charts.

From SRB, page 24

PROCEDURES

Have the group leaders pass out the SRBs. Ask students to open their books to the beginning (page 4) and look at the Starting Level Guide that they completed in the first week of the SRA READING LABORATORY program. Call students' attention to the first part of the SLG—the beginning inventory, where they recorded their reading habits, out-of-school activities, and so forth.

> ◆ **ON** the first day of our SRA READING LABORATORY work, you answered some questions in the Starting Level Guide. Now that you have worked with the multilevel system, let's read those questions again.

Allow a few minutes for students to read. Then, ask them to look at the final evaluation section on the last page of the SLG (page 7). Allow a few minutes for students to read over the six questions. Then, ask them to write their answers to the questions, answering each one as honestly and completely as they can.

When students have finished writing, have the group leaders collect the SRBs. Compare each individual's impressions and hopes at the beginning of the program with his or her evaluations and suggestions at the end. This analysis can show you how to work more effectively to help your students.

References and Resources

APPENDIX A: Holding Student Conferences and Interpreting Progress Charts

Holding Student Conferences

◆ To the greatest extent possible, your student conferences should be *cooperative* ventures in which you and the student reach a decision *together* regarding the student's performance. The student should be encouraged to help decide whether he or she is ready to advance to a new level or whether remaining in the current level awhile longer is appropriate. Students unused to having such responsibility for their own instruction and progress will probably be a little hesitant to join in the decision at first. Soon, however, they will become accustomed to the idea and will acquire considerable skill in analyzing their own work.

Occasionally, students will not want to advance because they enjoy the success they are having with the easier work. Then, you will have to prod them a little. On the other hand, there are always a few students who are *too* anxious to advance. You will tactfully have to slow them down, without destroying their enthusiasm. In either case, the Progress Charts are the basis for wise decisions.

In these conferences, students may reveal certain concerns. They may feel ashamed to make mistakes. If so, explain that it is natural to make mistakes and that mistakes can help you to learn, provided you take the time to find out why you made the mistake.

Students may be worried because of the irregular appearance–highs and lows–of their Progress Charts. Explain that there is no perfect progress from day to day. The important thing is the general direction in which one is moving.

The student may be worried about competition with others. Emphasize that students develop at different rates. The important thing is one's own development, one's own progress. The student who advances through the lower levels makes as much progress as the one who advances through the higher levels.

INTERPRETING PROGRESS CHARTS

◆ Here are some samples of typical progress charts with interpretations. A study of these will assist you in guiding students to evaluate their own work and program their own learning.

On the opposite page is a typical chart of an average learner.

❶ The student began her work in the Violet level. On her first three Power Builders, she recorded a declining percentage right in both comprehension and word skills—well below the acceptable 85 to 100 percent.

At the student's first conference, her teacher noted that she was working very quickly. (Note "Working Time" graph steadily dropping.) Apparently she considered the Power Builders some kind of speed test. After a brief discussion, the student decided that she had been working too rapidly.

❷ Having reviewed the Power Builder procedures during her follow-up work, and having taken the time to work carefully, the student improved in the next six Power Builders. Her percentage reached and then passed 85 percent. Now, she found that she could work somewhat faster. She and her teacher decided that she was ready to move to the next color level, Rose.

❸ On beginning the new level, the student naturally found the work more difficult. Her percentage right decreased. She remembered what happened earlier, however, so she took more time with the first Power Builders. She began to increase her percentage and reduce her working time until she was ready for a new level.

Power Builder Progress Chart: Average Learner

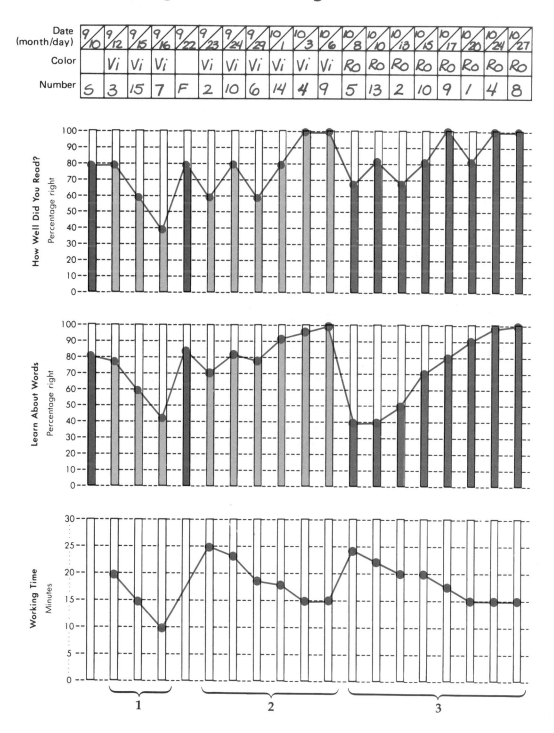

On the opposite page is a typical chart of a slow learner.

❶ The student began work in Brown, the lowest color level. On the first three Power Builders, his scores on the comprehension section were acceptable and showed progress, but his scores on the word-skill exercises were uniformly low.

At the student's first conference, his teacher noted this discrepancy. A quick check of the record pages indicated that he often made mistakes because he did not follow directions. For instance, he answered *long* and *short* rather than *yes* and *no.*

❷ Working more slowly and carefully, the student did eight more Power Builders. Slowly he progressed until his percentage right averaged between 80 and 100 percent. He and his teacher decided that he was ready to move on to the next level, Lime.

❸ The student's scores dropped when he began the new and harder work. He will probably need to do at least ten or eleven Power Builders in the Lime level before moving to the next level. Generally, slow students will need to do more Power Builders in each level, and will move through fewer levels than average or superior students.

Power Builder Progress Chart: Slow Learner

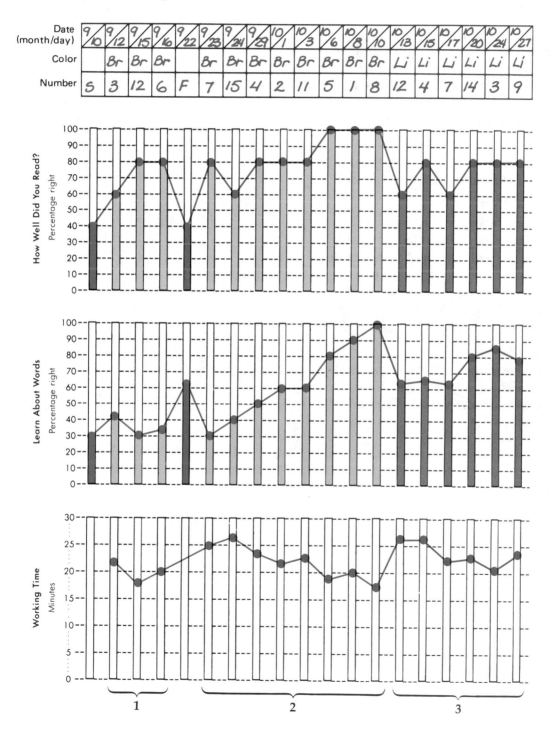

Date (month/day)	9/10	9/12	9/15	9/16	9/22	9/23	9/24	9/29	10/1	10/3	10/6	10/8	10/10	10/13	10/15	10/17	10/20	10/24	10/27
Color		Br	Br	Br		Br	Br	Br	Br	Br	Br	Br	Br	Li	Li	Li	Li	Li	Li
Number	5	3	12	6	F	7	15	4	2	11	5	1	8	12	4	7	14	3	9

On the opposite page is a typical chart of a superior learner.

❶ The student began work in the Purple level. She made good comprehension scores on the "How Well Did You Read?" section, but in her independent work on "Learn about Words," her word-analysis skills were somewhat lacking. She began to concentrate more on her word-analysis skills.

❷ Her comprehension scores held up well, and her word-analysis skills in the "Learn about Words" section showed definite improvement.

❸ After she had achieved a consistent 85 to 100 percent in three straight Power Builders, she and her teacher concluded that she was ready to move to a higher level, Violet. Her scores dropped when she entered the more difficult level, but after doing six Violet Power Builders, she was ready again to move to a higher level, Rose.

❹ Again her scores dropped at first, but will rise soon. The superior learner will usually do fewer Power Builders in each level and will move through more levels than the average or slow learner.

Power Builder Progress Chart: Superior Learner

Date (month/day)	9/10	9/12	9/15	9/16	9/22	9/23	9/24	9/29	10/1	10/3	10/6	10/8	10/10	10/13	10/15	10/17	10/20	10/24	10/27
Color		Pu	Pu	Pu		Pu	Pu	Pu	Pu	Pu	Vi	Vi	Vi	Vi	Vi	Vi	Ro	Ro	Ro
Number	S	1	15	3	F	4	9	13	2	6	5	2	15	12	8	4	4	15	6

How Well Did You Read? Percentage right

Learn About Words Percentage right

Working Time Minutes

1 2 3 4

HOW STUDENTS ARE DIFFERENT

◆ In an average class of thirty students, many levels of reading ability will be found, as indicated by the normal distribution curve shown. But, regardless of your students' present reading ability—at grade level, below grade level, or above grade level—*each* student can advance to a higher level when he or she has a multilevel learning opportunity.

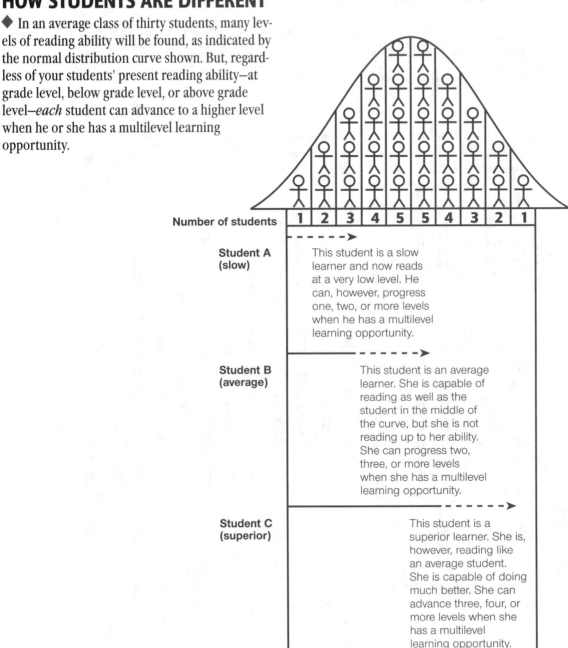

Number of students

| 1 | 2 | 3 | 4 | 5 | 5 | 4 | 3 | 2 | 1 |

Student A (slow)

This student is a slow learner and now reads at a very low level. He can, however, progress one, two, or more levels when he has a multilevel learning opportunity.

Student B (average)

This student is an average learner. She is capable of reading as well as the student in the middle of the curve, but she is not reading up to her ability. She can progress two, three, or more levels when she has a multilevel learning opportunity.

Student C (superior)

This student is a superior learner. She is, however, reading like an average student. She is capable of doing much better. She can advance three, four, or more levels when she has a multilevel learning opportunity.

Note: Even the superior student who now reads well above grade level may lack the skills needed for in-depth interpretation and the language facility emphasized in the upper levels of the SRA READING LABORATORY program.

Students enjoy sharing their Power Builder reading experiences with others at the same reading level, and can often work together on the "Use Your Imagination" enrichment activity.

Because the range of topics in the Laboratory's Power Builders is so wide, students can nearly always find material that appeals to their interests.

APPENDIX B: Answers to Frequently Asked Questions

When should the SRA READING LABORATORY program be started?

Teachers generally find it most desirable to schedule SRA READING LABORATORY work as early as possible in the school year. The increased reading efficiency built by the program then can be put to use in all school subjects for the greater part of the school year.

Why not spread the program across the entire school year?

Teachers sometimes ask why we recommend against spacing the program sessions more widely so that they occur across the entire school year. As was pointed out in the front of this Handbook ("Getting the Most out of the Program"), such spacing is not recommended because the principle of reinforcement does not operate well when the program sessions are spaced widely. When practice periods are close together, there is a carryover of learning from one day to the next. When practice periods are too far apart, there is greater risk that students will forget both the information learned and the procedures to follow. During the early stages of a learning process especially, practice is most efficient when closely spaced.

What if the class has used a Reading Laboratory before?

If the class used a *Reading Laboratory* kit last year, you will probably know at what levels the students completed their work. It is recommended, nonetheless, that you begin this year's program by administering the Starting Level Guide. If students' SRA READING LABORATORY work was completed early in the year, students will probably have continued to progress well beyond their finishing level, especially if they were trained to transfer the techniques they learned to other work.

If your pupils are familiar with the materials and procedures of the program, you will not need to spend as much time in introductory work. You might, for instance, elect to omit the Power Builder Follow-up in favor of additional Power Builder work. We recommend that you follow the teaching schedule on page 16 of this Handbook, whether or not the class has had previous experience with the program. In the second and third years, however, the program can be extended throughout the year after the training phase has been completed.

What determines the difficulty of the color levels?

Many things determine the difficulty of the color levels. A time-tested readability formula is used in conjunction with sensitive editorial judgment to control the average sentence length and vocabulary load of Power Builders. Vocabulary is, in addition, checked against widely accepted word lists such as *EDL* and *The Living Word* to ensure that the burden of unfamiliar words does not become excessive at any level. In addition, the length of the reading selections increases at every level, and the comprehension checks and word-skill exercises become more mechanically complex and demand increasingly sophisticated kinds of thinking. (For Power Builder lengths and the number of comprehension checks at each level, see the chart on the inside front cover of this Handbook.)

In a multilevel program, it makes little sense to ask if level 5.5 is where a student "ought to be reading" in the fifth month of fifth grade, and SRA discourages such literalism about reading levels. The multilevel philosophy holds that every student "ought" to be reading at the level where he or she experiences success—the level that provides the best stepping-stone to the levels yet to come. The beauty of the SRA READING LABORATORY system is that it provides *appropriate* material for every student in the classroom, no matter what the student's ability level, and it is the student's own success with the material that determines his or her placement at all times.

Because readability formulas and their usefulness are topics of renewed concern in the reading community, a more detailed discussion of this question is presented in Appendix C.

What about grading?

It is recommended that a student's work in the program be ungraded; the Progress Charts should tell the story. If students are reading successfully at a low level, but working up to their ability, is it fair to give them a poor grade? On the other hand, such students should not be led to consider themselves above average, only to find later that they are deficient in academic ability. If a grade is necessary, a dual grading system might be used—one grade for effort and another for realistic ranking of functional ability. Such a system might prove useful not only for slow students but also for superior students who do only average work because of lack of effort.

What about competition and cheating?

Competition and cheating are closely interrelated problems. If a student takes advantage of the Key Cards' availability to copy answers, or if the student otherwise falsifies his or her scores, it is probably done in an effort to keep up with other class members or to get ahead of them. The cultural patterns in some school communities are such that a student may feel ashamed at being in, say, the Purple level while friends are already working at Violet, Rose, or some higher level.

For this reason, it is important in the initial stages of the program to put across the idea that multilevel work does not involve a race among classmates—that different children *will be* in different color lev-

els because students differ, and the Laboratory kit provides materials that are right for each one.

It is also important to play down the idea that moving from one color level to another is the badge of success. This is *one kind* of success, which might be called vertical progress. But there is also horizontal progress—succeeding in each Power Builder one works within a level, as each Power Builder presents new skills to master or different approaches to similar skills. Students should therefore be encouraged to see their goal as one of simply working as well as possible with the materials that are right for them. They should not view climbing up the ladder of color levels as the goal of Laboratory work. Obviously, the teacher must play a key role in forming appropriate attitudes about what constitutes success.

Students defeat only themselves when they seek status among classmates by defeating the Laboratory's continuous placement mechanism and by moving ahead in the color sequence by means of copied answers or falsified scores. That student misses needed practice and ends up in material that is too difficult. A teacher can try to put this idea across, although obviously there will be resistance if a student has been taunted by a classmate for being "only in Blue," for example. The teacher then faces the traditional problem of how to get a student to do what's best in the long run when the student prefers to do what seems to provide immediate status and peer acceptance. It is a problem that occurs in all areas of child behavior when a competitive atmosphere exists, and it is by no means unique to the Laboratory situation. Teachers who have found ways to deal with it in other areas of school life will probably handle it successfully in connection with the Laboratory.

If cheating is apparent, a confidential talk with the student is a good idea. You can stress the idea that "one only cheats oneself" and help the student to understand that hurrying from level to level is not the aim of Laboratory work. Remember, too, that by spot-checking for errors and by praising accuracy and neatness in scoring, calculating, and charting, you can set up an atmosphere that discourages cheating.

Finally, remember that it is *not* cheating to look back at the story in order to answer the comprehension and vocabulary checks. Indeed, looking back should be encouraged as preferable to guessing or relying on uncertain recollections. Looking back is what we all do (and *should* do) in real-life reading situations when we want to be sure about what we have read. Once this is understood, some students may no longer have the need to misuse the Key Card or alter their scores.

What about record keeping?

Because the SRA READING LABORATORY program is learner-directed, the teacher enters no scores and corrects no papers, except for the Starting Level Guide. The student does all the necessary record keeping in his or her Student Record Book. The records each student maintains are invaluable guides to the diagnosis of his or her reading difficulties, progress, and long-range educational potential. Many schools, therefore, retain the covers of the Student Record Books and pass them along to the students' new teachers at the start of the next school year. Thus, the new teachers have a complete record of what level each student started in, how many levels each progressed, and how well he or she did in each part of the program. Eventually, these records are placed in each student's personal folder.

The value of these student-kept records is threefold: (1) In parent counseling, the Progress Charts form an objective basis for interpreting school progress in the vital area of reading. They provide a direct and unbiased reflection of the student's day-to-day work. (2) In pupil guidance, the Progress Charts represent a cumulative record of the student's actual *functional* ability to learn through reading. Such information is useful in helping both the parent and the teacher or guidance worker—as well as the student—in planning the student's educational future realistically. (3) In curriculum improvement, analysis of the functional reading levels of pupils may indicate to the teacher or curriculum worker a need for revising upward or downward the difficulty level of offerings in the various subject areas. Such a study might point out a need for further steps toward individualizing learning opportunities.

"SQR" and "Learn from Your Mistakes" are effective techniques to help students monitor and improve their own learning strategies.

Using group leaders to pass out the Power Builders and Student Record Books is an option to consider if you want to reduce classroom traffic to and from the Laboratory box.

APPENDIX C: The Role of the Readability Formula in the SRA READING LABORATORY Series

◆ Readability formulas have come in for some well-deserved criticism that parallels what SRA has long been saying. Thoughtful educators recognize that merely manipulating the number of words, syllables, and sentences in a text cannot, by itself, guarantee the suitability of that text for any given grade or child. There are too many variables that formulas cannot measure.

SRA knows what can happen when formulas are applied mechanically and without sensitivity. Altering a text to make it "easier" by formula, for example, might actually make it harder for a child to comprehend. This can happen if essential connective words are eliminated to shorten sentences or if the *best* word to express an idea is changed to a shorter but less exact word. When these things happen, readability formulas simply produce bad writing.

An oft-repeated example of this abuse is the case of the textbook that retold the story of "The Shoemaker and the Elves" without ever using the words *shoemaker, elves,* or even *shoes.* The resulting text was virtually incomprehensible except by strenuous inference from its illustrations.

These problems should not be found in the SRA READING LABORATORY Series. SRA has been keenly aware of the limitations of readability formulas for over three decades, having worked with them ever since the first *Reading Laboratory* kit was published in 1957. SRA views readability formulas with a healthy realism, considering them useful guides for predicting readability in a general way; they are convenient first checks. But they can never be the last word or a substitute for informed judgment.

APPENDIX D: Interest Areas Covered by Power Builder Selections

◆ To give you an appreciation of the scope of interests covered in a *Reading Laboratory* kit, here is a list of interest areas that SRA seeks to cover in a balanced fashion. The coverage ranges from sports and lighthearted fiction to information about the highest cultural achievements of mankind—always written in a manner that young readers can understand and relate to.

Literary Heritage Great authors and great stories that include retellings and excerpted scenes from the classics, biographical selections about great writers, and the sources of expressions and concepts that we use in everyday speech.

Inspiring Persons Factual articles about individuals of all races who have demonstrated character, conviction, and achievement.

Human Society Factual and fictional selections dealing with the social aspects of human life—including our customs, institutions, human relationships, work, clothing, food, entertainment, and the insights of the social sciences.

Interesting Places and People The lure of foreign lands and the fascination of divergent cultures as revealed in factual articles and realistic fiction.

Traditional Tales Fiction and fictionalized fact from long ago and far away—often with an embedded teaching or moral. Includes folklore, legends, and myths that have been used by various cultures to explain the world.

Fun and Fancy Jokes, riddles, light humor, whimsical fiction, and true anecdotes primarily for amusement and amazement.

The Sciences Factual selections dealing with physical science, earth science, and life science and the men and women who pursue these studies.

Discovery Factual selections dealing with how humankind has broadened its knowledge—how new lands, new ideas, and new understandings of the world have become known and have altered our physical and mental landscape.

Technology Factual selections dealing with the results of human ingenuity in applying science and invention to solve problems and enhance the quality of life.

Real Animals Factual selections about particular species and their often fascinating appearance, abilities, and life habits.

Animal Personalities Selections depicting individual animals as characters; includes the "humanized" animals of lighthearted fiction as well as true stories of affectionate relationships between people and animals. This category embraces factual selections, fanciful fiction, and realistic fiction.

Sports Factual and fictional selections appealing to the young reader's love of athletics and contests of skill; includes biographical selections about sports heroes.

Adventure Factual selections and realistic fiction appealing to the reader's taste for action, excitement, and daring.

Mystery Factual and fictional selections in which the primary appeal is the solving of a puzzle. This category can include the solving of a scientific mystery by dedicated researchers as well as the solving of a crime or other mystery by police or detective work.

Fine Arts Factual selections dealing with painting, music, sculpture, architecture, dance, and other artistic endeavors; includes biographical selections about men and women of achievement in these fields.

APPENDIX E: Complete List of Power Builder Titles, Authors, and Sources

3.0 Aqua

1 *The Rooster and the Fox*
retold for SRA from the fables of Aesop

2 *Does a Dog Talk?*
by Dr. Michael W. Fox
adapted from *Ranger Rick's Nature Magazine* (National Wildlife Federation)

3 *Born to Dance*
by Clare Coverdale

4 *Warning! Black Holes*
by Pamela Conrad

5 *Changes in the Sky*
by Mae and Ira Freeman
adapted from *The Sun, the Moon, and the Stars* (Random House)

6 *Food for the Gods*
an original article written for SRA, based on the myths of ancient Greece and Rome

7 *The Horse Who Could Count*
by Helen Kay
adapted from *How Smart Are Animals?* (Basic Books)

8 *Statues That Walk*
by Chris Williams

9 *Trouble Dolls Save the Day*
by P. J. Luecke

10 *The Cuckoo*
by Malcolm Carrick
adapted from *The Wise Men of Gotham* (Viking)

11 *The Storyteller of Cross Creek*
an original article written for SRA, based on the life of Marjorie Kinnan Rawlings

12 *Can Ants Talk?*
by Dorothy Van Woerkom
adapted from *Wee Wisdom* magazine

13 *Aloha! Hello and Good-Bye*
by Anna Dale

14 *Her Father's Songs*
by Ana Christos

15 *The Milkman and the Monkey*
by John W. Spellman
adapted from *The Beautiful Blue Jay and Other Tales*

3.5 Blue

1 *The Ungrateful Tiger*
a folktale from India
retold by Irene Geesicke

2 *Where Did the Sun Go?*
by Franklyn M. Branley
adapted from *Eclipse, Darkness in Daytime* (Crowell)

3 *Kristi Yamaguchi's Golden Goal*
by Trent MacLane

4 *Harriet Tubman*
by Johanna Johnston
adapted from *A Special Bravery* (Dodd, Mead)

4.0 Purple

4.5 Violet

6.0 Orange

7 *The Farmer's Wife and the Tiger*
by Ikram Chunghtai
adapted from *Folk Tales from Asia for
Children Everywhere*
(Asian Cultural Center for UNESCO)

8 *Do It Yourself!*
by Suzanne Seed
adapted from *Saturday's Child*
(Book Trading)

9 *The Pineapple*
by Wilma P. Hays and R. Vernon Hays
adapted from *Foods the Indians Gave Us*
(Ives Washburn)

10 *The Treasure of Sumiko's Bay*
by Barbara Chamberlain
adapted from *Jack and Jill* magazine
(Saturday Evening Post Company)

11 *Four Children Who Created a World*
an original article written for SRA, based on
the lives of Charlotte, Emily, Anne, and
Branwell Brontë

12 *Clementine Hunter, American Folk Artist*
by Elinor Lander Horwitz
adapted from *Contemporary American Folk
Artists* (Lippincott)

13 *A Game of Chinese Jump Rope*
by Elizabeth Lane

14 *Inside a Bird's Egg*
by George Laycock
adapted from *Boys' Life*
(Boy Scouts of America)

15 *Rescue Mission*
by Colonel Carroll V. Glines, Jr.
adapted from *Helicopter Rescues*
(Scholastic Inc.)

7.0 Gold

1 *Learning to Be a Steamboat Pilot*
adapted for SRA from *Life on the Mississippi*
by Samuel L. Clemens (Mark Twain)

2 *"Tell Them about the Time—"*
by Sandra Fenichel Asher
adapted from *Young World* magazine
(Saturday Evening Post Company)

3 *The Comical Kea*
by Beth Day
by permission of John Hawkins & Associates, Inc.

4 *A Jigsaw Puzzle*
by Malcolm E. Weiss
adapted from *Lands Adrift*
(Parents' Magazine Press)

5 *Courage*
by Joanne Mitchell
adapted from *Young World* magazine
(Saturday Evening Post Company)

6 *Mayday! Mayday! Crash in Space*
by Wiley Blevins

7 *Cheryl Toussaint, Track Star*
by Francene Sabin
adapted from *Women Who Win*
(Random House)

8 *Bill Pinkney's Incredible Voyage*
by William O'Farrell

9 *The Stranger*
by J. D. Woods
adapted from *School Magazine*

8.0 Brown

APPENDIX F: Comprehension and Word Study Skills Charts

Aqua 3.0

Comprehension "How Well Did You Read?"	Power Builder Number														
	1	2	3	4	5	6	7	8	9	10	11	12	13	14	15
Cause/effect					●	●		●		●					
Sequence															
Problem/solution	●											●			
Main idea															
Character			●												●
Setting/mood				●							●				
Comparison/contrast		●													
Purpose/conclusion							●		●				●	●	

Word Study "Learn about Words"		Power Builder Number				
		1 6 11	2 7 12	3 8 13	4 9 14	5 10 15
Sections A and B Questions 1–10	Vocabulary: word meaning from context	●	●	●	●	●
	Vocabulary: using word in new context	●	●	●	●	●
Section C Questions 11–18	Consonant blends: br, cr, dr, fr, gr, pr, tr, tw, nd, nt, nk, mp	●				
	Consonant clusters: scr, str, spr, spl, thr, squ, qu		●			
	Base word plus endings: 's, s' (possessives)			●		
	Consonant diagraphs: ch, sh, ph, th, gh				●	
	Word classification					●
Section D Questions 19–26	Vowel combinations: aw, ay, au, ai	●				
	Compound words		●			
	Adjectives: comparative, superlative			●		
	Vowel combinations: ai, oa, ay, ow				●	
	Homographs					●
Section E Questions 27–33	Contractions	●				
	Study skills: using guide words in a dictionary		●			
	Study skills: choosing correct encyclopedia volume			●		
	Alphabetical order: second letter				●	
	Alliteration					●

Blue 3.5

Comprehension "How Well Did You Read?"	Power Builder Number														
	1	2	3	4	5	6	7	8	9	10	11	12	13	14	15
Cause/effect		●	●			●									
Sequence					●					●					●
Problem/solution	●							●							
Main idea											●				
Character				●					●			●	●		
Setting/mood														●	
Comparison/contrast															
Purpose/conclusion							●								

Word Study "Learn about Words"		Power Builder Number				
		1 6 11	2 7 12	3 8 13	4 9 14	5 10 15
Sections A and B Questions 1–10	Vocabulary: word meaning from context	●	●	●	●	●
	Vocabulary: using word in new context	●	●	●	●	●
Section C Questions 11–18	Short/long vowels plus *r*-influenced *a, e, i, o, u*	●				
	Soft and hard *c*		●			
	Base word plus endings: *s, ing, ed* (verbs)			●		
	Nouns				●	
	Verbs					●
Section D Questions 19–26	Vowel combinations: *ow (cow), ee (feed)*	●				
	Soft and hard *g*		●			
	Adjectives: comparative, superlative			●		
	Noun markers: *a, an, the, every, my, your, his, her, its, our, their*				●	
	Question markers: *do, does, did*					●
Section E Questions 27–33	Study skills: choosing correct encyclopedia entry	●				
	Vowel combinations: *ou (out), ow (low)*		●			
	Study skills: using a dictionary pronunciation key			●		
	Synonyms				●	
	Homographs					●

Purple 4.0

Comprehension "How Well Did You Read?"	Power Builder Number														
	1	2	3	4	5	6	7	8	9	10	11	12	13	14	15
Cause/effect								●							
Sequence															
Problem/solution							●		●					●	●
Main idea										●					
Character	●				●	●									
Setting/mood															
Comparison/contrast				●							●		●		
Purpose/conclusion		●	●									●			

Word Study "Learn about Words"			Power Builder Number				
			1 6 11	2 7 12	3 8 13	4 9 14	5 10 15
Sections A and B Questions 1–10		Vocabulary: word meaning from context	●	●	●	●	●
		Vocabulary: using word in new context	●	●	●	●	●
Section C Questions 11–18		Silent consonants: k, w, l, b	●				
		Sound of wh		●			
		Nouns (regular and irregular)			●		
		Verbs				●	
		Synonyms					●
Section D Questions 19–26		Vowel sound of oo as in look; oo as in noon	●				
		Sounds of y		●			
		Noun markers: a, an, the, every, my, your, his, her, its, our, their			●		
		Sentence patterns: N-V, N-V-N				●	
		Similes					●
Section E Questions 27–33		Study skills: bar graph	●				
		Study skills: interpreting a table		●			
		Homographs			●		
		Question markers: who, what, where, when, why				●	
		Vocabulary in context area					●

Violet 4.5

Comprehension "How Well Did You Read?"	Power Builder Number														
	1	2	3	4	5	6	7	8	9	10	11	12	13	14	15
Cause/effect		●					●		●				●	●	
Sequence								●							
Problem/solution			●			●									
Main idea				●	●										
Character	●									●		●			
Setting/mood															●
Comparison/contrast															
Purpose/conclusion											●				

Word Study "Learn about Words"		Power Builder Number				
		1 6 11	2 7 12	3 8 13	4 9 14	5 10 15
Sections A and B Questions 1–10	Vocabulary: word meaning from context	●	●	●	●	●
	Vocabulary: using word in new context	●	●	●	●	●
Section C Questions 11–18	Prefixes: *pre, dis, mis*	●				
	Noun-marking suffixes: *ist, hood, ness, ship*		●			
	Verbs			●		
	Forms of *be*				●	
	Synonyms					●
Section D Questions 19–26	Prefixes: using in context	●				
	Identifying subject and predicate		●			
	Linking verbs			●		
	Jumbled sentences				●	
	Antonyms					●
Section E Questions 27–33	Study skills: line graph	●				
	Study skills: using a card catalog		●			
	Verbs (irregular and past tenses)			●		
	Sentence patterns: *N-V, N-V-N, N-LV-N*				●	
	Vocabulary in context area					●

Rose 5.0

Comprehension "How Well Did You Read?"	Power Builder Number														
	1	2	3	4	5	6	7	8	9	10	11	12	13	14	15
Cause/effect													●		
Sequence															
Problem/solution			●											●	
Main idea												●			
Character	●					●		●		●	●				●
Setting/mood		●													
Comparison/contrast															
Purpose/conclusion				●	●		●		●						

Word Study "Learn about Words"		Power Builder Number				
		1 6 11	2 7 12	3 8 13	4 9 14	5 10 15
Sections A and B Questions 1–10	Vocabulary: word meaning from context	●	●	●	●	●
	Vocabulary: using word in new context	●	●	●	●	●
Section C Questions 11–18	Prefixes: *in, im, mis*	●				
	Noun-marking suffixes: *ment, or, er, ion, ant, age*		●			
	Noun-marking suffixes: *age, ant, ance, ence*			●		
	Sentence patterns: *N-V, N-V-N, N-LV-N*				●	
	Antonyms					●
Section D Questions 19–26	Latin prefixes: *inter, super, sub*	●				
	Identifying subject and predicate		●			
	Suffixes: using in context			●		
	Synonyms				●	
	Antonyms: constructing with affixes *dis, un, ir, in*					●
Section E Questions 27–33	Prefixes: using in context	●				
	Study skills: map reading		●			
	Homonyms			●		
	Study skills: using an index				●	
	Metaphors					●

Red 5.5

Comprehension "How Well Did You Read?"	Power Builder Number														
	1	2	3	4	5	6	7	8	9	10	11	12	13	14	15
Cause/effect															
Sequence															
Problem/solution		●								●			●		
Main idea			●	●			●								
Character					●										
Setting/mood								●	●						
Comparison/contrast						●						●			●
Purpose/conclusion	●										●			●	

Word Study "Learn about Words"		Power Builder Number				
		1 6 11	2 7 12	3 8 13	4 9 14	5 10 15
Sections A and B Questions 1–10	Vocabulary: word meaning from context	●	●	●	●	●
	Vocabulary: using word in new context	●	●	●	●	●
Section C Questions 11–18	Prefixes: *in, re, pre*	●				
	Helping verbs		●			
	Adjectives			●		
	Synonyms				●	
	Personification					●
Section D Questions 19–26	Prefixes: using in context	●				
	Verb-marking suffixes: *en, ate, ify*		●			
	Adjective-marking suffixes: *en, ful, ic, ish*			●		
	Antonyms				●	
	Antonyms: constructing with affixes *dis, un, ir, in, counter*					●
Section E Questions 27–33	Latin roots: *rupt, volv, vis, mot, script*	●				
	Study skills: dictionary entries—multiple meanings (parts of speech)		●			
	Onomatopoeia			●		
	Synonyms, antonyms: using in context				●	
	Study skills: using a dictionary pronunciation key					●

Orange 6.0

Comprehension "How Well Did You Read?"	Power Builder Number														
	1	2	3	4	5	6	7	8	9	10	11	12	13	14	15
Cause/effect		●										●		●	●
Sequence									●						
Problem/solution				●											
Main idea															
Character			●		●	●	●			●					
Setting/mood															
Comparison/contrast								●							
Purpose/conclusion	●										●		●		

Word Study "Learn about Words"		Power Builder Number				
		1 6 11	2 7 12	3 8 13	4 9 14	5 10 15
Sections A and B Questions 1–10	Vocabulary: word meaning from context	●	●	●	●	●
	Vocabulary: using word in new context	●	●	●	●	●
Section C Questions 11–18	Prefixes: re, de, be, en	●				
	Adjective-marking suffixes: y, ive, able, ly		●			
	Sentence patterns: N-V, N-V-N, N-LV-N, N-LV-Adj.			●		
	Pronouns				●	
	Noun-marking suffixes: ion, ist, er					●
Section D Questions 19–26	Prefixes: using in context	●				
	Suffixes: using in context		●			
	Noun phrases			●		
	Pronoun referents				●	
	Synonyms					●
Section E Questions 27–33	Latin roots: pel, tort, mit, liber, creat, capt	●				
	Study skills: bar graph		●			
	Jumbled sentences			●		
	Study skills: line graph				●	
	Antonyms					●

Gold 7.0

Comprehension "How Well Did You Read?"	Power Builder Number														
	1	2	3	4	5	6	7	8	9	10	11	12	13	14	15
Cause/effect												●			
Sequence															
Problem/solution					●										
Main idea	●			●							●				
Character		●	●			●	●		●	●			●	●	●
Setting/mood								●							
Comparison/contrast															
Purpose/conclusion															

Word Study "Learn about Words"		Power Builder Number				
		1 6 11	2 7 12	3 8 13	4 9 14	5 10 15
Sections A and B Questions 1–10	Vocabulary: word meaning from context	●	●	●	●	●
	Vocabulary: using word in new context	●	●	●	●	●
Section C Questions 11–18	Adjective-marking suffixes: *al, ous, y, less*	●				
	Adverbs		●			
	Latin roots: *fer, rupt, mot, struct, vis*			●		
	Verb phrases				●	
	Pronouns					●
Section D Questions 19–26	Latin roots: *flex, dict, habit*	●				
	Adjective-adverb markers: *very, rather, somewhat, more, most, too*		●			
	Homonyms			●		
	Helping verbs				●	
	Pronoun referents					●
Section E Questions 27–33	Study skills: diagram	●				
	Study skills: map reading		●			
	Antonyms			●		
	Sentence patterns: *N-V, N-V-N, N-LV-N, N-LV-Adj.*				●	
	Synonyms					●

Brown 8.0

Comprehension "How Well Did You Read?"	Power Builder Number														
	1	2	3	4	5	6	7	8	9	10	11	12	13	14	15
Cause/effect					●		●				●	●			●
Sequence										●					
Problem/solution		●	●												
Main idea													●		
Character	●					●		●						●	
Setting/mood															
Comparison/contrast															
Purpose/conclusion				●					●						

Word Study "Learn about Words"		Power Builder Number				
		1 6 11	2 7 12	3 8 13	4 9 14	5 10 15
Sections A and B Questions 1–10	Vocabulary: word meaning from context	●	●	●	●	●
	Vocabulary: using word in new context	●	●	●	●	●
Section C Questions 11–18	Noun-marking suffixes: *er, ment, or, ation*	●				
	Latin prefixes: *counter, non*		●			
	Greek word parts: *chrono, bio, psycho, geo, logy, path, meter, stat, thermo, hydro, aero*			●		
	Prepositional phrases				●	
	Synonyms					●
Section D Questions 19–26	Suffixes: using in context	●				
	Latin word parts: *semi, ped, lun, equi, cent, lat, annu*		●			
	Latin roots: *dict, press, tract, gress, creat, capt, flex*			●		
	Prepositions: using in context				●	
	Antonyms					●
Section E Questions 27–33	Study skills: line graph	●				
	Homonyms		●			
	Study skills: bar graph			●		
	Conjunctions				●	
	Euphemisms					●

Tan 9.0

Comprehension "How Well Did You Read?"	Power Builder Number														
	1	2	3	4	5	6	7	8	9	10	11	12	13	14	15
Cause/effect								●		●					
Sequence					●								●		●
Problem/solution							●								
Main idea									●		●	●			
Character	●			●		●								●	
Setting/mood		●													
Comparison/contrast															
Purpose/conclusion			●												

Word Study "Learn about Words"		Power Builder Number				
		1 6 11	2 7 12	3 8 13	4 9 14	5 10 15
Sections A and B Questions 1–10	Vocabulary: word meaning from context	●	●	●	●	●
	Vocabulary: using word in new context	●	●	●	●	●
Section C Questions 11–18	Latin roots: *ject, scribe, spect, fer, sect, vert*	●				
	Adjective-marking suffixes: *ly, y, less*		●			
	Greek word parts: *philo, gamy, graph, syn, anti, homo, phon*			●		
	Noun clauses				●	
	Adjective-marking suffixes: *ful, y, less*					●
Section D Questions 19–26	Latin word parts: *sol, aqua, son, ocul, per*	●				
	Appositives		●			
	Metonymy			●		
	Adjective clauses				●	
	Conjunctions					●
Section E Questions 27–33	Homonyms	●				
	Metonymy		●			
	Study skills: diagram			●		
	Study skills: using reference aids				●	
	Metonymy					●

Starting Level Guide for **Reading Laboratory® 2c Kit**

Beginning inventory of

Last name   First name   Middle initial   Date

Teacher _____ School _____ Grade _____

1 I can read as well as I would like to. ☐ Yes ☐ No (Check one.) If you checked *No,* complete all the statements below. If you checked *Yes,* skip 2 and 3, but complete 4, 5, and 6.

2 I would like to read better because I _____

_____

3 I think the reasons that I do not read as well as I would like to are _____

_____

4 The kinds of things I like to read best are _____

_____

5 The things I like to do best in my spare time are _____

_____

6 When I complete my schooling, I want to _____

_____

7 I have used an SRA READING LABORATORY kit before. ☐ Yes ☐ No (Check one.)

If you checked *Yes,* what grade were you in when you used it? _____

Here is a little story to read. After the story, you will find some questions. First, read the story; then read the questions and choose the *one best* answer to each question. When you find the answer, put its letter in the correct box on the right side of the page. While you are answering the questions, you may look back at the story if you wish. Use a SMALL letter to write your answer in the box.

Example

Did you ever see a porpoise walk on its tail? A man has trained a porpoise to do this on command. The big fishlike creature leaps almost out of the water. Then, he begins to move his tail rapidly. Faster and faster he goes, across the top of the water. Then, with a splash, Mr. Porpoise swims away.

1 A man has trained a porpoise to .... ☐
  a fly   **b** eat fishlike creatures   **c** walk on its tail on command   **d** swim away

2 When the porpoise walks on its tail, it is .... ☐
  a under the water   **b** on top of the water   **c** eating fishlike creatures   **d** training a man

■■■ STOP HERE ■■■

Story A

Who was the first person to go 100 miles an hour? It was Charley Hogan. The year was 1893. He was picked to pilot the *999*. It was the first train engine ever built to go 100 miles an hour–maybe more.

The sleek, black giant quickly hit 80, then 90. The countryside whizzed by in a blur. "She's had it!" yelled the firefighter.

"Not yet," cried Charley. "Shovel more coal!"

Charley pushed the throttle another notch. The wheels screamed. The engine leaped forward like a mad monster. He watched the hand move up . . . 95 . . . 100 . . . 105 . . . and finally to 112 ½. He'd made it and then some.

The news swept the world. The *999* became the most famous engine of all time. It was shown at several world's fairs. Charley always went with it. He was now a world-famous engineer.

1 Charley Hogan was .... ☐
   a an airplane pilot   **b** a truck driver   **c** a railroad engineer

2 The engine ran on .... ☐
   a gasoline   **b** coal   **c** electricity

3 When the 999 reached 90, the fireman wanted to .... ☐
   a go faster   **b** slow down   **c** get off

4 The engine went .... ☐
   a faster than expected   **b** slower than expected   **c** off the track

5 Charley .... ☐
   a never piloted the engine again   **b** always went with his engine   **c** let the firefighter run the engine

━━━━━━━━━ **STOP HERE** ━━━━━━━━━

Name _____

Total right, Story A _____

Total right, Story B _____

Total SLG score _____

Story B

The digital computer was developed in the late 1930s. Since that time, the computer has profoundly affected everyone. It helps predict elections, guide astronauts, control traffic, forecast weather, compute bank statements, and does hundreds of other tasks unheard of a generation ago.

But even familiar devices like the washing machine, the telephone, and the stoplight are computers in their own right. They have the same basic elements of operation: input, processing, and output.

For the washing machine, the input is dirty clothes (and detergent), the processing is washing the clothes, and the output is the same clothes–clean.

For the computer, input consists of a program and data. In processing, the computer uses the program to operate on the data–to solve an equation, for example. Output is the solution.

The computer programmer can instruct a machine to add, subtract, multiply, divide, and do dozens of other actions in any sequence. But an adding machine or calculator can add, subtract, multiply, and divide. Why is the computer so great?

One reason is speed. The computer makes it possible to tackle problems so large as to be impossible the pencil-and-paper way. For example, to do all the adding a computer can do in ten seconds would take a person more than a hundred days. And that's allowing no time for sleeping, eating, or pencil sharpening.

Some have said that the computer will make it unnecessary for humans to think. People who program a computer must think very clearly to get the computer to do the work they want it to do. And that's the key to the relationship of humans with computers. Let the computer do the work it can do best. Humans are then free to think about how to live together in peace–a kind of "thinking" a computer could never do.

1 The digital computer was developed .... ☐
   a several centuries ago   **b** only a few months ago
   c in the late 1930s   **d** in the seventeenth century

2 The computer affects .... ☐
   a everyone   **b** most people
   c a few special people   **d** no one

3 Computers are similar to .... ☐
   a washing machines   **b** telephones
   c stoplights   **d** All of these

4 A computer and a washing machine both have .... ☐
   a input   **b** data
   c detergent   **d** All of these

5 A computer and a telephone both have .... ☐
   a input   **b** processing
   c output   **d** All of these

NOW GO ON TO THE NEXT PAGE

6 Programmers .... □
  a let the computer tell them what to do   **b** tell the computer what to do
  c are faster than the computer   **d** are part of the computer

7 If an adding machine can add, subtract, multiply, and divide, why use computers? .... □
  a Computers can do the job in one hundred days.   **b** Computers can print out the answers.
  c Computers can work with very big numbers.   **d** Computers are faster.

8 The story says that a good programmer .... □
  a must think clearly   **b** lets the computer do the thinking
  c lets the computer work alone   **d** uses common sense

9 Implied but not stated: .... □
  a Computers think, but humans cannot.   **b** Computers can solve any problem.
  c Humans think, but computers cannot.   **d** People who program computers must think.

━━━━━━━━━━━━━━━ **STOP HERE** ━━━━━━━━━━━━━━━

Final evaluation of _____ Date _____
                    Last name   First name   Middle initial

Teacher _____ School _____ Grade _____

Give your frank and honest opinions on the questions below:

1 Do you like the reading work you have been doing with *Reading Laboratory 2c* kit?

  □ Yes   □ No   (Check one.)

2 What have you learned from this work so far? _____

_____

3 Has your reading work helped you in doing other schoolwork? If so, how? _____

_____

4 What did you like best about your work with *Reading Laboratory 2c* kit? _____

_____

5 What particular thing did you like least about this work? _____

_____

6 What suggestions can you give for making the READING LABORATORY program even better? _____

_____

Dear Parent,

In the coming months, your child will be involved in using the SRA Reading Laboratories. Perhaps you remember the Reading Labs from your own school experience. For many years, the SRA Reading Labs have been an enduring classic in classrooms across America and around the world.

This 1996 edition of the Reading Labs contains a wealth of new reading selections. Your child will be reading biographies of contemporary figures such as Linda Ronstadt, Morgan Freeman, and Olympic skater Kristi Yamaguchi. There are stories and articles that cover a range of topics, from surfing the Internet to unusual scientific phenomena. There is folk literature, and there are selections from the classics of world literature.

You may find that your child will want to learn more about the different people and topics encountered in the Reading Labs. You can encourage further reading by taking your child on trips to the library and by sharing your child's excitement at making new discoveries.

The SRA Reading Labs have provided opportunities for successful reading experiences to generations of American readers. We hope that the Labs will be a starting point for your child as he or she journeys into the world of reading.

Index

Notes